E.R5

Hormone Jungle

Hi Elizabeth!

Brod Bagert
2013

Brod Bagert

Hormone Jungle
Coming of Age in Middle School

Hormone Jungle: Coming of Age in Middle School
by Brod Bagert

Cover and Book Design: Mickey Cuthbertson
Editor: Erica Nikolaidis

Library of Congress Cataloging-in-Publication Data

Bagert, Brod.
  Hormone jungle : coming of age in middle school / Brod Bagert.
     p. cm.
  Summary: College-bound Christina Curtis is creating a scrapbook of the
Digital Poets, her middle-school poetry group, which, interwoven with her
narrative, reflects the hormonal angst of middle school.
  ISBN 0-929895-87-8
  [1. Middle schools--Fiction. 2. Schools--Fiction. 3. Dating (Social
customs)--Fiction. 4. Poetry--Fiction. 5. Death--Fiction.] I. Title.
  PZ7.B14022Hor 2006
  [Fic]--dc22
                                   2005013934

ISBN-10: 0-929895-87-8
ISBN-13: 978-0-929895-87-1

The Publisher thanks Alexandria Zettler's middle school art class at P.K.Yonge Laboratory School in
Gainesville, FL for the student artwork in *Hormone Jungle*.

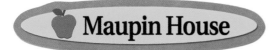

Maupin House Publishing, Inc.
2416 NW 71st Place
Gainesville, FL 32653
Phone: 800-524-0634 Fax: 352-373-5546
www.maupinhouse.com / email: info@maupinhouse.com

Publishing Professional Resources that Improve Classroom Performance

Putting this book together is the very last thing I ought to be doing the summer before I go to college. I can't explain it to myself, let alone to you, but it's something I have to do. I guess it's because of Steven Gilley. It's been almost three years since we last spoke, and I thought I was over him, but I was wrong.

It's all because of the box of poems I found stashed in the back of my closet. They were written by me and my friends when we were in middle school. I opened the box, looked at the top page, and there it was: my first poem, the poem that started it all. I knew without even looking that the next page would be a poem written by Steven. As I read it, I started laughing and crying at the same time. He always had that effect on me.

Don't think about him, I thought to myself, but it was too late. There was already a memory running through my head like a movie. We're in seventh grade, the second year of the Digital Poets. Steven Gilley is sitting across from me in the library, and for the hundredth time we're having the same argument.

I say we can't keep publishing every poem that's submitted; it's time to get more selective. Steven responds by saying that many of us feel rejected most of the time, and that writers have to start somewhere. For three years we worked together as coeditors of what we called the Digital Poets, for three years we had the same argument, and for three years Steven got his way.

Sitting on the floor of my closet, I realized that if I did a scrapbook now I could pick the poems I liked best, and Steven wouldn't be here to argue about it. Then I heard a voice inside me—*Oh, Steven, if only you were here*. That's when I knew I had to do it, because of him. I never dreamed I'd be saying this, but Steven Gilley was one of the best things that ever happened to me, and I felt like maybe, if I made this scrapbook, I'd be able to put it all behind me so I could go on with the rest of my life.

So here it is. It's not a big deal, like a novel or anything; just a few of our poems and the story of how we became the Digital Poets.

Contents

Meet The Digital Poets

I decided to put these introductions at the beginning because I prefer to know something about poets before I read their poems. If you're like me, you'll probably want to start here.

You may be one of those people who would rather read the poems first. If so, please skip this part and start with "A Poetry War: Athena versus Thor" on PAGE 8

CHRISTINA CURTIS

This is me—simple, honest, straightforward, alluring, and near perfect in every way. Oh, and I almost forgot. Humble.

ISABELA GALINDO

It was easy to be Isabela's friend as long as you did what she told you to do, and did things her way. If you looked at her genes under a microscope, her DNA chain would have spelled the word "BOSS." If you were ever in an argument, Isabela was the person you wanted on your side.

Her personality would have driven you crazy if it weren't for the fact that she was one of the most generous people I have ever known. Anything she possessed she was willing to share, except her boyfriends, and she always seemed to have several strung like pearls around her ankle.

STEVEN GILLEY

The thought of Steven Gilley, the mere mention of his name, produces inside me a storm of memories and mixed feelings. It's impossible for me to sum it all up in a paragraph or two, but I can say this:

Steven Gilley was often the most annoying, ridiculous, obnoxious person imaginable, which is how our poetry war got started in the first place. He was also gentle and wise and profoundly thoughtful, which is why he became the closest friend I ever had. He remains to this day my very favorite poet.

BOBBY HALL

Bobby Hall's poems are always about him getting flattened on the football field and landing in the hospital. The interesting thing is that he made it all up. Bobby was an incredible football player. He may not have liked me putting it this way, but watching him run with a football was like watching a ballet dancer. It's almost as though he used his poems to make fun of his own inner fears. I don't know, but I like them. I think it's pretty cool that our golden boy of the gridiron had a perverse fascination with the idea of getting smushed.

AMY HAYS

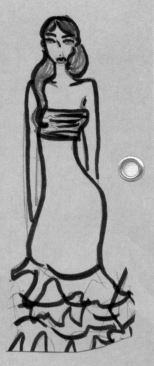

Amy stood out in a crowd—literally. She was six feet tall in sixth grade, with high cheekbones, exotic eyes, and a dynamite figure. But she wasn't at all self-conscious about her appearance. With Amy, what you saw was what you got.

She was one of those people who seemed to be good at everything, and it wasn't just natural talent. Amy worked hard at whatever she did, and what she did best was play basketball. Yes, basketball was her life. Basketball and Gerald T. Adams, that is.

JUAN CARLOS HERNANDEZ

I can't say anything about Carlos without first telling you that he had a pet tarantula. Actually, he started out with three tarantulas but two of them died when the pest control guy sprayed too close to their aquarium. Carlos was so upset that he missed two days of school. So the thing about Carlos is that he was painfully sensitive, which you'll see in at least one of his poems.

ASHLEY HUFFMAN

Although Ashley didn't write her own poems, she deserves a place on this page because she made our poems come to life. Ashley Huffman was the ultimate performer. She needed to perform like she needed air, and she was magnificent.

It was Ashley's dramatization of "Middle School Payback" that incited the original poetry war; it was Ashley's brazen confrontation with Mr. Barker that started Free Choice Poetry; and it was Ashley's enthusiasm for dramatic interpretation that inspired many of us to write. I remember moments when, in the middle of composing a poem, I'd stop and imagine how Ashley would sound reciting my words, almost as if I were writing for her to perform.

EMMA MACKEY

Emma once described herself as an "air-headed boy-crazy blonde Aquarius," but she was also the smartest person in middle school. She loved riding horses and wanted to train them for a living. She once told me that if you can handle horses, you can handle boys.

Emma looked at life through a microscope; always observing, always analyzing, as though, if she thought hard enough, the world would start to make sense. Emma was a puzzle. She always acted like everything was going great, like she was really happy, but you got the feeling that there was something else going on—like there was a storm inside her. She never talked about it, but it was always there.

SHAYNA POTTS

Shayna was definitely Irish. She had a huge mop of curly red hair, emerald green eyes, and an attitude that could give you third degree burns. From the very first day of school it was clear that Shayna was on a mission to drive our teachers crazy, never missing an opportunity to explain why they were wrong about everything.

Shayna marched to the beat of her own drummer. In sixth grade she wore purple eye shadow, in seventh grade she dyed her hair black, and in eighth grade she got her naval pierced. She was also the kind of friend who was always there when you needed her and never talked behind your back.

GERALD T. SIMPSON

The phrase "never judge a book by its cover" was written with Gerald-T in mind. He looked like a grizzly bear but inside he was Teddy bear from head to toe.

In this book you'll find only three poems by Gerald T. Adams, but that's not because he didn't write more. He wrote lots of poems, twice as many as any of us, but almost all of them were about eternal love and devotion to his "adorable" Amy Hays. The three poems I picked are my favorites. They show how Gerald-T truly respected and appreciated girls, starting with his mother, which I still think is a very cool thing.

RYAN SPALDING

Whenever I think about Ryan Spalding, even now, I start to laugh. And it's not like he tried to be funny. He could walk into a room and everybody would start to laugh, laughing at him and with him at the same time.

He loved to make fun of himself and he did it constantly—how he'd go out for football if only he could learn to hold the ball and run at the same time, or how he was born with the head of a spider monkey and the ears of a bull elephant. If you were waiting for Ryan to drop the act and be himself, you'd have to wait a long time. Ryan was always exactly what he appeared to be.

BENJAMIN TALKINGTON SPROCK, III

Benjamin Sprock never owned a single pair of jeans. He wore slacks to school every day, and carried his books in a briefcase. In seventh grade he tried to start a young Republicans club and was surprised when nobody wanted to join.

Now I don't want to give you the wrong impression. Benjamin was a nice person and I liked him, but he had certain habits that were annoying, like posing. It's hard to explain, but he forever acted as if someone were about to take his picture and he spent more time fixing his hair than most of the girls.

Speaking of girls—Benjamin was chronically girl-crazy. He really thought he was some kind of Romeo. One of his friends claimed that he actually practiced lines in front of the mirror. I am happy to report that he never tried his lines on me, which is probably the best thing I can say about him.

A Poetry War:
Athena versus Thor

I was on the phone with Ashley Huffman, and she was ranting about how sixth grade boys were totally uncivilized, how they never paid attention to us, and how someday they'd be sorry. "Girl," she said, "It won't be long till I'll look like the goddess of love and those boys will be like frogs croaking at my feet."

I told her I thought it was best just to ignore them, but that sent Ashley into full drama-mama mode. "Ignore them!" she shouted. "How exactly do you ignore boys? Last week when I had that huge pimple on the end of my nose, that new boy, Steven Gilley, called it 'Big Red' and started interviewing it. 'Well, Big Red,' he said, 'what's it like to be a zit sitting on the end of Ashley's nose.' Christina, how do you ignore something like that?"

She was right of course. It was impossible to ignore Steven Gilley. He was the kind of boy who made fart jokes when girls wore perfume. He was unbearably immature, totally annoying, and absolutely typical of the herd of mule-headed males that passed for human beings in sixth grade.

Like the surge of tidal flood waters that come right before a hurricane, angry feelings about the Steven Gilleys of the world began to rise inside me, and that's when it happened. The sound of an angry voice, the universal voice of the sixth grade girl fed up with the pestilence of male immaturity, began to form in my head. I sat down and wrote my first poem.

I read the first draft and realized that I needed a pen name. Ashley's comment about the goddess of love gave me the idea of writing in the name of a goddess, but not a goddess of love. What I needed was none other than Athena, the warrior goddess of wisdom and strength. Perfect!

The next day I went to school early and got on a computer in the library. I rewrote the first draft of my poem, made some final changes, printed a bunch of copies, and plastered one on the door of every classroom in the sixth grade hall. Athena the Warrior Goddess was born.

Middle School Payback

You boys are so immature.

The things we girls put up with.

The things we've put up with since kindergarten.

You called us names,

Excluded us from games,

And now you expect us to be sweet.

Oh yeah, now we're looking good.

Oh yeah, now you really need us.

And sure, now you're trying to be nice.

Well it's too little, too late,

So suffer, dog!

This ain't elementary anymore,

You're in a brave new world,

You're a boy in middle school

And buster, I'm a girl!

So down on your knees and crawl, slime,

Middle school is payback time.

I will never forget how it felt to watch people react to my poem. Most of the girls read it and laughed, but not Ashley Huffman. She didn't just read it; she actually became Athena the Warrior. For the rest of the day, every time she saw a boy, she'd shout, "On your knees, SLIME!" and wave her arm in command like it was a scepter. The boys hated it. The girls loved it. And for two days the entire sixth grade talked about nothing but Athena the Warrior and wondered who she really was. For two days girls ruled, but on the third day a new poem appeared, plastered not just on classroom doors but on every wall in the school. It definitely was *not* written by a girl.

To: The Sixth Grade Boys
From: Thor the Hammer God

Romantic Appetite

She says when she sees me
Her heart starts to quicken,
But all I can think of
Is crispy fried chicken.

She says when I speak
Her brain starts to quake,
But my brain is quaking
For fries and a shake.

She says I'm the sun
And the moon in her sky,
But all I can think of
Is hot apple pie.

I try to be nice,
I try not to be rude,
But talking to girls
Makes me think about food.

So wash off that lipstick,
Who cares how you look?
If you want my attention
Just learn how to cook.

And if, as you say
You really do need me,
Stop talking about it,
Just get up and feed me!

"Get up and feed me?" Who was this male chauvinist? Did he want to be bottle-fed, spoon-fed, or have his meal fist-first? I was furious and so was every other girl in the class. And the boys? The way they carried on was disgusting. Even though I secretly admitted to myself that Thor was a pretty good writer, I vowed that he would not get away with this. The next day Athena struck again.

To: Thor the Male Chauvinist Pig
From: Athena the Warrior Goddess

Eggs and Bacon

He thinks that I need him,

He says I should feed him?

That chauvinist pig is mistaken.

The way that I feel,

If I cooked him a meal,

I'd fry eggs and use *him* for the bacon.

I figured that would put Thor back in his place, but it didn't, at least not for long. It was poetry war!

To: Athena the Doberman Puppy
From: Thor the Hammer God

Puppy Poet

Little pincher, little biter,

Feisty little poem writer,

You gave me such an awful bite,

Why do you always have to fight?

A poem that calls a boy a hog—

Such a naughty puppy dog.

Thor was holding his own. I didn't like what he said, but he did say it well. And he was funny to boot. I hated that I was actually starting to like him. More and more I wondered who he was, but I didn't have to wonder long.

It happened in the middle of English class. The voice of the principal boomed over the intercom, "Christina Curtis and Steven Gilley, report to my office immediately." I froze in my seat as every eye seemed glued to me. I knew I was in big trouble and figured it had to do with the poems being taped all over the walls. Then it hit me: if the principal thinks I'm Athena, he must think Steven Gilley is . . . I looked at Steven and knew it was true; Steven and Thor the Hammer were one and the same, and at that particular moment the Hammer looked as worried as I felt.

Julius Augustus Dulabaum had been the principal of middle school forever. The man was a legend, and if you were called to his office you were sure to remember it. It was like appearing before the Spanish Inquisition. For fifteen minutes we waited nervously outside his office. Each minute seemed like a year, but when the door finally opened it was Mrs. Zimmerman, the school librarian, who came out and not Mr. Dulabaum.

"There is no need for you to report to the principal," she said. "I have spoken on your behalf and the matter has been resolved."

"How? What?" we stammered at the same time.

"Your questions will be answered soon," she said as she stepped into the hallway. "Now, please follow me."

A few minutes later the three of us were sitting at a table in the library. "I take my job very seriously," she said, "and, if I must say so myself, I do a good job of managing the resources entrusted to me. Those resources include the library computers and by now you should know that you cannot use a computer in my library without me being aware of it."

Steven Gilley groaned as Mrs. Zimmerman continued with a smile. "I've known all along who was writing those poems and I have thoroughly enjoyed your work. So when Mr. Dulabaum discovered it was you, I simply told him that you had my approval. I admitted that neither of you actually knew you had my approval, but I insisted that as educators we couldn't let technicalities stand in the path of emerging literature."

I wanted to ask what she meant by "emerging literature" but she didn't give me a chance.

"Look around you," she continued. "This is the poetry section. The men and women who wrote these books were just like you. Like you, they had feelings and fears and hopes and dreams. Like you, they struggled to understand who they were and how they fit into the world around them. And like you, when they felt the need to share their struggles with others, words took shape inside of them and flowed onto paper in a river of poetry."

Then she leaned forward and looked each of us in the eye. "You're poets," she said, "and you're publishing your work. That's what literature is all about. So congratulations . . . and thank you."

Mrs. Zimmerman was a piece of work. She had just saved our butts and she was thanking us. I was relieved, but Steven Gilley still looked worried.

"Do we have to stop?" he asked. "I mean I know we can keep writing, but do we have to stop putting them on the walls?"

"You cannot continue papering the hallways all over the school, but perhaps the wall outside the library door can be designated as a Poetry Wall. Yes, I think that might do quite nicely."

The Sixth Grade Poetry Wall seemed like a good idea, but it didn't work out so well. Right from the start students began drawing pictures on the poems. Some of the artwork was cool, but some of the pictures weren't so cool. For example, when Emma Mackey wrote "Horses and Boys," someone drew a horse's rear end and labeled it "Emma." There was also a space problem; it didn't take long for half the class to write at least one poem and the wall soon became a mess. Mrs. Zimmerman said there was a solution for every problem and, as it turned out, the solution came from an unexpected direction.

Benny Giles was a computer geek. He was addicted to a ridiculous internet war game that had teams and tribes. The players in each tribe were all over the country, so to keep everything organized there were tribe websites. Benny had taught himself to design websites just so he could be the webmaster for his tribe. I thought the whole thing was absurd, but I was delighted when Benny surprised us with our own website. He hadn't consulted anyone about it; he just did it, and it was perfect. Well, almost perfect—I didn't like the name. Benny called it www.DigitalPoetsInTheHormoneJungle.com. Most of us thought we could come up with a better name but Benny loved it. No one wanted to hurt his feelings, and the name stuck. We even started calling ourselves the Digital Poets.

After all the problems we'd had with the poetry wall, we decided we needed rules for our website. Mrs. Zimmerman said we needed only three: 1) No more pen names; 2) Be sensitive to the privacy and feelings of others; and 3) No cursing. She also said we needed a committee to look at the poems and make sure the rules were followed before they went online.

Students submitted their work on a disc to the committee, which met once a week, reviewed the poems, and made a master disc for Benny to upload to the website.

Everything was running smoothly, except we couldn't get people to work on the committee. Most of the time it was just Steven Gilley and I. Sometimes I wondered if I hadn't made a terrible mistake.

Athena
vs.
Thor

Our Sixth Grade Poems

The Gap
by Emma Mackey

I'm a sixth grade girl, I'm young and free,
And you'll never see a boy sitting next to me.

I'm a sixth grade girl and I'm here to say,
I'm glad that boy's sitting far away.

In sunshine or rain, no matter the weather,
Me and that boy ain't sitting together.

But love is like a mysterious trap,
Because day by day we are closing the gap.

Great Minds
by Shayna Potts

Mrs. Wiley's English class,
Our first test of the year,
And every one of us bombed it
Except Harry Higginbotham
Whose mind, it would seem,
Runs in perfect sync with Mrs. Wiley.

Question #1:
In Rudyard Kipling's Rikki
Tikki Tavi,
What was the cobra thinking?
Higginbotham's Answer:
Cobras do not think.
Mrs. Wiley's comment:
Not what I was anticipating,
But OK, correct.

Question #2:
Was Rikki Tikki Tavi a hero?
Higginbotham's Answer:
No. He was a mongoose.
Mrs. Wiley's comment:
I'm beginning to see how you think,
Correct again.

Question #3:
   Would you recommend this story to your
   friends?
Higginbotham's Answer:
   Yes
   If they did not have to answer
   A bunch of ridiculous questions.
Mrs. Wiley's comment:
   Oh Mr. Higginbotham,
   I couldn't agree with you more.
   ABSOLUTELY CORRECT!

And how did Mrs. Wiley explain herself?
   "Comic actor, tragic clown,
   Great minds flying upside-down,
   The human brain is lots of fun,
   So open yours and let it run."

Now we know
For the rest of the year
Taking tests in English class
Will be more fun than anyone ever expected.
And we agree with Mrs. Wiley:
   Comic actor, tragic clown,
   Great minds flying upside-down,
   Human brains need lots of fun,
   So open yours and let it run.

COUNTY PUBLIC LIBRARY

Friends by Juan Carlos Hernandez

Eric Reed is my friend:
> He acts real crazy wherever he goes,
> He picks in his ears, he picks his nose.
> He wants lots of money but won't work to earn it,
> He borrows my stuff and forgets to return it.
> His shoes are scuffed, his hair's a mess,
> But in spite of it all I must confess,

Eric is my best friend.

And I'm not so perfect myself:
> My disposition is seldom sunny,
> My practical jokes are not so funny.
> I lose my temper and start to yell,
> If I know a secret I usually tell.
> I lick my fingers, I lick my plate,
> If I'm going to meet you I'm usually late.

But Eric? He likes me anyway.

You may never find two better friends,
Though you search both near and far,
Because Eric and I accept one another
Exactly the way we are.

Lips

by Ryan Spalding

"Zachary Bloom's my very best friend!"
I used to say it with pride,
And every thing we ever did
We did it side by side.

But now the earth is inside-out,
My life is in a twirl,
Because today I learned the truth,
Zachary . . . kissed . . . a girl!

Ug! Yuck! Disgusting!
Beat me with a stick!
He actually kissed her on the lips,
It's enough to make you sick!

Everything we ever did
We did it two by two,
So does that mean the time has come,
I'll have to kiss one too?

Ug! Yuck! Disgusting!
It's enough to make you hurl,
I'LL NEVER, NEVER, NEVER,
NEVER, NEVER KISS A GIRL!

Torture Queen
by Shayna Potts

It's like she's an evil queen,
And school is her domain.
Our teacher's only happy
When she's causing lots of pain.

First, in social studies,
That's when we knew our fate.
She made us learn the capital
Of every single state.

In science she looked wicked,
Her face turned hard as granite,
"Now," she said, "We'll learn the names
Of every single planet."

But none of us could yet foretell
The fury of her wrath.
Yes, that would be revealed to us
The day we started Math.

Long division, ratios,
Decimals and fractions,
Katie shouted, "Stop it please!
I can't control my actions."

Then Katie started groaning,
She crawled around the floor,
And the whole school heard her howling
As she darted out the door.

The Torture Queen just smiled.
She was happy as could be,
Evil-bound she loved the sound
Of pain and misery.

No Reason at All

by Shayna Potts

Back in third grade,
When I was still small,
I was mad at the world
For no reason at all.

I was mad every day.
I was mad all night long.
I was mad to be right.
I was mad to be wrong.

Mad at my enemy,
Mad at my friend,
Mad at the start,
And mad at the end.

But now I'm all grown
And ever so clever,
I'm bigger and smarter
And madder than ever.

So why am I angry?
I cannot recall.
But I'm mad at the world
For no reason at all.

Internet Lies
by Steven Gilley

I met her last night
Somewhere in the cyber chat room,
She sat at her keyboard and typed:

My name is Lola.
I'm twenty-five years old.
Five feet four inches tall,
With red hair and green eyes,
And I am a professional dancer.

So I, a sniveling sixth grade boy, replied:

Hi, Lola,
I'm Chuck.
I'll be twenty-eight next week,
I'm six-foot-four,
Two hundred and forty pounds,
And I'm a body builder.

Then with each new message,
Our hearts, like rosebuds,
Blossomed into cyber love.

That was last night,
But today at the mall,
I overheard Agnes Ripple,
Nine-year-old, fourth-grade, skinny-to-the-bone Agnes Ripple.
She was giggling about Chuck,
The body builder she met last night on the Internet.

I said, "Hello Lola! I'm… Chuck?"
But instead of the fire that was once in her eyes,
I saw only the ashes of our cyber space lies.
So I made up my mind, for the rest of my life,
In the real or the cyber space world,
I will almost never tell a lie
When I'm falling in love with a girl.

Planning for the Future

by Benjamin Talkington Sprock, III

I've been thinking,
And I have decided that I like women:
    I like the way they look,
    I like the way they sound,
    I like the way they smell.

But the girls in sixth grade
Are not exactly women yet:
    They've got pimples,
    They sound screechy,
    And they smell like wet dogs.

But I treat them nice anyway:
    I say, "Your hair looks nice today."
    And, "I'd sure like to hear *your* opinion."
    Or, "Is that a new perfume?"

In a few more years these skinny girls
Will be women one and all,
And for a guy like me it's going to be
Like I'm shopping at the mall.

Horses and Boys
by Emma Mackey

My name is Emma Mackey
I'm twelve years old,
And I like horses—
    They're stubborn,
    They're stupid,
    And they stink,
But I like horses.

I also like boys—
Ditto.

Aunt Aurora's Promise

by Shayna Potts

I don't think Daddy likes her,
He says she's really wild,
Just because she dresses
With her own Aurora-style.

She never ever wears her hair
The way my Daddy likes,
She uses lots of gooey stuff
And shapes it into spikes.

Her lips are painted purple
And her nails are painted black,
So Aunt Aurora looks as though
She's ready to attack.

So Daddy's feeling nervous,
He's feeling full of stress,
Cause Aunt Aurora promised me
She'd teach me how to dress.

The Dance
by Emma Mackey

It was a disaster.
    The boys ran around all night
    (I think they were playing tag),
    While the girls stood patiently and watched.
    But we didn't get angry.
    Those poor little boys,
    It's such a hard time for them.

Like Shirley Ryan's boyfriend Jonathan.
    She's five-foot-two
    And he's only four-six and a half,
    And the last time they danced
    His hair got tangled in her braces.

And Peter Castansa can't dance.
    He doesn't have a sister,
    How can a guy learn to dance
    If he doesn't have a sister?

And the rest of them are scared to death.
    They see how nice we look
    And how nice we smell
    And they're scared that if they get too close
    We'll cast our feminine charms like a spell
    And make them love-slaves for life.

So for now the boys can run and play tag,
But the future's a matter of fate,
Sooner or later they'll crawl at our feet
And we girls have the patience to wait.

Yuck!
by Amy Hays

I've got a few questions
And I'll make it real quick
'Cause the mere thought of kissing
Is making me sick.

Do you pucker your lips
Or make your lips soft?
And what do you do
If your throat needs to cough?

Do you hold your breath
Till your eyes start to pop?
How long must you wait
Before you can stop?

This learning to kiss
Is a horrible task,
Some questions are just
Too disgusting to ask.

So answer me please,
And please make it quick
'Cause the mere thought of kissing
Is making me sick.

Freedom of Speech
by Shayna Potts

I feel no guilt, I feel no shame,
It's not my fault, I'm not to blame.
How could I be such an awful fool?
There's no free speech for a kid in school.
        "Do you like your classes?" my principal said,
        And my mouth started working instead of my head.
        "I hate the quizzes, I hate the tests,
        Recess is what I like the best.
        I hate my classes, I hate my books,
        And I'm not too cool on my teacher's looks."
It's not my fault, I feel no shame,
My principal's the one to blame.
Freedom of speech is seldom clear cut
So I'm learning to keep my big mouth shut.

Twenty-Five Hours
by Gerald T. Simpson

I've never seen her so angry:
    "Gerald T. Simpson,
    I'm telling you for the last time,
    Clean your room.
    No!
    Last time *was* the last time.
    YOU ARE GROUNDED!"
I tried to explain:
    I was in class all day,
    Wrestling practice all evening,
    Tonight I had a mountain of homework,
    And I couldn't go to bed without talking to Amy.
I tried to explain but my mother wouldn't listen.

So I wrote my mother a little note
Attached to a bouquet of flowers,
"I would have cleaned my room today
If today had had twenty-five hours."

The Hunt
by Benjamin Talkington Sprock, III

I try hard not to be negative,
But it's very difficult to ignore the fact
That girls are totally irritating!
And, if you're a boy, they never leave you alone.

They whisper behind your back,
They talk about who you like and who likes you,
They write little notes and hide them from us,
And if you tell them you don't care about their stupid notes
They play like their feelings are hurt
And tell everybody how mean you are.

In the classroom, in the lunchroom,
On the bus or on the phone,
Girls hunt boys like we're animals
And they never leave us alone.

The Moment of Silence
by Emma Mackey

Another Friday night:
    Talking about the same old things,
    Watching the same old scary movies,
    Eating the same greasy, pepperoni pizza.
Totally boring.

Then it happened.
My friend Leah jumped out of her chair,
Clicked off the TV,
And howled,
    "Nathan Brokaw,
    I cannot live without you!
    I need you,
    I love you,
    I will call you on the phone."
This is more like it,
I thought as I ran to the extension phone,
Waited for her to dial,
Lifted the receiver,
And listened for the sweet sound of Nathan's voice.

But Nathan's voice did not answer.
And the voice that did answer was not sweet.
It was the voice of a grizzly bear.
It was the voice of a gorilla.
It was the voice of Nathan's father.

"It's one o'clock in the morning,
Who is this?" he growled.

I hung up the phone and tried not to imagine
The fun we could have had,
If only Nathan had answered the phone
Instead of Nathan's dad.

Queen of the Beasts
by Christina Curtis

I fell across my bed and cried,
I was very, very sad.
"Why the tears?" my sister said,
"It can't be all that bad."

I told her I asked if he'd like to hang out
To share a little time.
And how he said he'd rather hang out
With a monster made of slime.

"Don't tell anyone what he did," I said
"And please don't say I cried.
Deep down inside he's very nice,
He could be if he tried."

My sister gave me a little hug,
Then she wiped away my tears,
"I know it's hard," she said to me,
"Just wait a few more years.

Because, little sister, it won't be long,
He'll do whatever you please,
He'll bring you candy and flowers,
He'll grovel on his knees.

It'll hit him like a thunderbolt
Just when he expects it the least.
That boy's just one of the animals,
And you will be Queen of the Beasts!"

Free Choice Poetry

By the time we were in seventh grade, poetry had become a part of everyday life. Everyone was reading, writing, and talking about the poems on the Digital Poets website, especially Ashley Huffman.

Ashley Huffman never wrote a poem in the entire three years of the Digital Poets, but she could recite and act out our poems at the drop of a hat. We called her "Drama Mama" because she loved to act and had already decided she would be a movie star one day. Whenever we put on a play, Ashley took center stage with the best part, and she made the most of it. She was really good.

It was Ashley's ranting about boys on the telephone that inspired me to write as Athena the Warrior, it was Ashley who provoked Steven Gilley to write in the voice of Thor, and it was Ashley who prompted what eventually came to be known as Free Choice Poetry. Ashley and crazy Mr. Barker, that is.

Mr. Barker looked more like a professional wrestler than a seventh grade English teacher, but he loved to recite poetry. He was always telling us that you had to read poetry out loud to really enjoy it. Every day at the beginning of class he would announce the poem of the day, recite it for us, and pass out copies for us to put in our poetry notebooks.

But "recite" doesn't actually describe what he did. On the day he "recited" Edgar Allen Poe's "Annabelle Lee," he started out speaking very quietly and then little by little got crazier until at the end he was a raving, hissing maniac. It was scary and funny at the same time. At first we thought he might be weird and didn't know how to react. Eventually, we came to understand that he really was weird, but we liked him anyway.

During class one day in the middle of fall semester, Mr. Barker announced that he'd discovered a new contemporary poet. "Her work

has been published only recently," he added, "but it's quite good, and I want you to become familiar with it so you can follow her literary career. The poem I've selected to recite is written in the voice of a seventh grade girl. It is called 'Complicated' by Christina Curtis."

My brain drained. I couldn't think. I couldn't swallow. *Is this some kind of joke,* I wondered? But it wasn't a joke. Before our very eyes, this huge, hairy man turned into a seventh grade girl. He stood like a girl, he moved like a girl, he even made his voice *sound* like a girl. He finished the poem, took a bow and everybody went wild, clapping and cheering. Everybody, that is, except Ashley Huffman. When the classroom quieted down, Ashley stood up and respectfully informed Mr. Barker that he had done it all wrong.

Mr. Barker raised one eyebrow and gave Ashley the teacher-look. "Well Ms. Huffman, why don't you just come up here and show us how to do it right?"

"Well, Mr. Barker, if you insist," she said smugly. Then she waltzed to the front of the room, turned to the class, and executed an extremely dramatic bow. All of us began clapping and howling and laughing. Ashley nodded approvingly, raised her hand to silence her audience, and began to perform.

I could never tell you how unbelievably good she was. When she finished and the applause finally stopped, Mr. Barker turned to her and said, "Miss Huffman, I bow to the master."

Ashley's performance had broken the ice. After that everyone wanted to perform. Paul Hastings performed "Lips." Sarah Anderson performed "Counter Intelligence." Eric Reed put on a Latino accent and performed "The Messenger." Finally, Mr. Barker said it was time to get back to work, but we didn't want to stop. It was "Just one more," and "Come on, Mr. Barker," and "Pleeeeeease." Mr. Barker promised we could do it again at the end of the week, and that was the beginning of Free Choice Poetry.

From then on, every Friday, anyone who wanted to could get up and perform one of their poems, or someone else's. Mr. Barker said it was best to memorize the poems, but he always let us hold a copy in our hands in case we got stage fright and went blank.

Poetry wasn't the most important thing in our lives, but it had become fun, something we cared about. This poetry wasn't just solving puzzles written by dead guys; it was about us, stuff we wrote, and instead of having to figure out what it meant, we figured out how to perform it.

It also began to affect our writing. Writing a poem was different when you knew it was going to be published on a website, in that someone might like it enough to perform it. The two Ps—publish and perform. Our poetry was coming alive.

It was a very cool year. Everybody talked about how good our poems were, how well we performed them, and how much fun we were having. Looking back, I think the eighth graders must have been a little jealous because for the whole year seventh grade ruled. Until, of course, a year later when *we* were the eighth graders and eighth grade ruled once again.

Middle School

Our Seventh Grade Poems

The Girl-Crazy Alien Body Snatcher
by Ryan Spalding

I have no idea when it started,
But lately I find myself actually attracted to girls.
Like yesterday,
Marilou Monahan smiled at me and said hello.
That was it.
One smile, one hello,
And my heart started beating like a bongo drum.

I know it sounds crazy,
And I hate to admit it,
But it's like there's this alien creature inside me,
And he likes girls,
And he's taking over my body.

But it's not going to happen,
Not if I have anything to say about it.
You won't see me talking sweet and holding hands,
But this crazy alien has other plans,
And he's trying to take control.
He's already got my body,
And now he's after my soul.

Complicated
by Christina Curtis

Ashley said:
"Omigawd!
He's so fine!
You have got to fix me up."

So I went up to him
And I said,
"If my friend Ashley thought you were cute,
Would you ever go out with her?"

But he said no,
He thought Ashley was a geek,
But I didn't tell her that,
I just said,
"He's already got a girlfriend."

But later,
Ashley saw him talking to Megan,
And Ashley assumed Megan must be his girlfriend.
So Ashley had Kitty call him on three-way
While Ashley listened in,
And he said, "Megan is not my girlfriend."
He said, "I like Christina."

Well I'm Christina,
And now Ashley is angry with me.
"Of course he's got a girlfriend,"
She shouted,
"You're his girlfriend!
Why didn't you tell me?
I feel like such a fool!"

I told her I had no idea he liked me,
But she didn't believe it,
And now she won't talk to me.
My best friend since kindergarten
And she won't even talk to me.
And it's not her fault,
It's his fault,
It's all his fault.
Boys!
They make everything so complicated.

Wailing Woman

by Emma Mackey

la la love you ...

I must be going crazy.
From the second I wake up in the morning
Till the second I go to sleep at night,
All I think about is boys:
     How Manuel is so romantic,
     How Kenny is so cool,
     How Andy's eyes are blue as the skies,
     How Eric makes me drool.
Has somebody cast a spell?

Yesterday I was a little girl,
Playing with my toys,
But today I'm a wailing woman
And I'm wailing about boys.

Yellow Bus Blues
by Shayna Potts

I think I shall always remember,
No matter where I roam,
The lovely moments we once shared
On the school bus riding home.

> I remember that autumn evening.
> As I tried to take a nap,
> Oliver Lee looked up at me
> And threw up in my lap.

> And Larry Hooper's girlfriend,
> As pretty as you please,
> Put nine kids in a coma
> The day she cut the cheese.

> That's when the driver hit the brakes
> And cried out with a wail,
> "Someone get me off this bus!
> I'd rather live in jail."

Oh yes, I'll always remember,
No matter where I roam,
Those wonderful moments we once shared
On the school bus riding home.

Hormone Madness
by Steven Gilley

I'm changing every day,
I'm changing head to toe.
My body's not the same
As it was a year ago.

It's like deep down inside of me
My hormones are at war.
I'm finding hair in places
Where it's never been before,
And my face is sprouting pimples
Out of every single pore.

And how should I behave?
There's no consistent rule.
All the stuff we did last year,
This year it isn't cool.

Some days I may seem happy,
But I'm seldom what I seem.
I'm smiling on the outside,
But inside I want to scream.

Will it be like this forever?
I really need to know.
Nothing is the same
As I was a year ago.

The Messenger
by Juan Carlos Hernandez

Eric Reed, my best friend, was in love with Rebecca.
I know because I got involved.
  "Please, Carlos," Eric pleaded,
  "Please deliver this note to Rebecca."
I should have run like a yellow dog
But, fool that I am,
I found Rebecca,
Gave her the note,
And started to walk away,
But she stopped me.

Rebecca

"Wait while I read it," she said with a smile.
Then she opened the note
And whispered the words:
> "My darling Rebecca,
> For far too long
> I have feared these simple words.
> But now, at long last,
> I have found the courage to say
> I love you.
> As the stars shine,
> As the moon glows,
> As the sun is light to the living earth,
> I love you."

I kept expecting her to end with something like
"Sincerely, Eric," or "Yours truly, Eric,"
But she never did,
Because Eric forgot to sign the note,
And before I could say a word
Rebecca was hugging *me*,
And saying how she loved me too.

"I know, I know it was all my fault,"
Eric said with a groan.
"I will never again send a friend to do
What a man ought to do on his own."

Man Fan
by Gerald T. Simpson

Thursday night basketball,
Hillcrest vs. Stapleton,
No place in the world I'd rather be.

    I love the rumble of the crowd
    As we stumble through the door.
    I love the smell in the air
    And the shine on the floor,
    And I love that Hillcrest center—
        Amy Hays, six feet tall,
        Finest center of them all.

That's why I'm here at every game,
A loyal Hillcrest man.
The center's name is Amy,
And I'm her biggest fan.

Jungle of Love
by Ryan Spalding

Cathy asked Megan if she liked me,
And she said she thought I was nice.
Then Cathy asked me if I liked Megan,
And I said I thought she was nice.

Then Cathy told me what Megan said,
And Cathy told Megan what I said,
And Cathy told everybody what both of us said,
And now everybody says
That Megan and I are going out.

It's like when they catch a tiger in the movies.
They dig a hole
And cover it up with grass,
And the tiger comes along,
Minding its own business,
And swoosh,
It's trapped at the bottom of a pit.

So watch out for girls,
Stay far away,
And when they ask questions,
Watch out what you say.

Because once I was free
Like a beautiful dove.
Now I'm trapped like a tiger
In the jungle of love.

¡No lo sé!

by Isabela Galindo

No lo sé, No lo sé.
It's what I always heard him say.

I'd ask:
"Eduardo, do you think I'm pretty?"
And he would answer:
"No lo sé."

I'd ask:
"Eduardo, do you like me?"
And he would answer:
"No lo sé."

I'd ask:
"Eduardo, tomorrow after school,
Could you walk with me to the mall."
And he would answer:
"No… lo… sé."

So this morning I broke up with Eduardo.
And at lunch Sam smiled at me,
And after school Ernesto asked to carry my books,
And on the bus Alan sat beside me.

And then tonight Eduardo called:
"¿Isabela," he cried,
"Querida mía Isabela,
Por qué rompes mi corazón?"

And that was when
It was my turn to say,
"¡Lo siento, Eduardo,
PERO NO LO SÉ!"

Talent Torture
by Steven Gilley

Last night I dreamed about Danny Groff:
  I made him run barefoot on hot coals,
  I made him swim in a pool of boiling oil,
  I made him kick a cement soccer ball.
It was pretty horrible,
But Danny deserves it.

Danny's not a bad guy.
It's just that he's great at every thing he does.
  He's the captain of the track team.
  He swims anchor for the relay team.
  And in soccer?
  He's the highest scoring forward in the history of the world.

My ego needs some polish,
But Danny's ego gleams.
So all day long I bear the pain,
And get even in my dreams.

Plain English
by Christina Curtis

Daddy?
Why can't you understand?
    I'm not *going out* with William,
    We're not even *dating*,
    We're just *talking*.

    And the movie with Matthew?
    That wasn't a *date*.
    We're *just friends*.
    How could I have a *date* with a *friend*?

    Besides I'm still *going out* with Oliver,
    But I heard that Oliver was *checking out* Monica,
    So I started *asking around*,
    And Shayna said that William's *sweatin' me*,
    And that's why I went to the movie with Matthew,
    So William would know I was about to *break up* with Oliver,
    And we could start *to talk*.

    And it worked like a charm:
    William and I are *talking*,
    Oliver knows *it's over* between us
    And he's starting *to talk* with Monica,
    Who *broke up* with William last week.

I am talking simple English,
The language of the land,
So Daddy, please explain to me,
What can't you understand?

Christina

Unwritten Rules
by Benjamin Talkington Sprock, III

TOO MANY RULES!

Sometimes I have no clue what's going on.
Like last night with Roxanne:
 "Oh Ben,
 I want to say I LIKE you,
 But it seems strange.
 It's like, if you said that you LIKE me,
 I think I'd say I LIKE you too."
So I said:
"Cool, Roxanne."
And she started to cry.
Then this morning Krystal attacks me:
 "Benjamin, how can you be so mean to Roxanne,
 Don't you know she LIKES you?"
And when I told her what Roxanne said
She went ballistic:

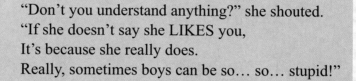

"Don't you understand anything?" she shouted.
"If she doesn't say she LIKES you,
It's because she really does.
Really, sometimes boys can be so… so… stupid!"

She actually called me stupid.
And why?
Because Roxanne and Krystal
And all the other women in the world
Have made up a bunch of rules
And they don't tell us what they are,
And they change them all the time,
But they expect us to know,
They expect us to read their minds,
And if we don't, we're stupid.

Girls make me crazy,
They make me feel like a clown.
They make a lot of rules,
But they never write them down.

Inner Eye
by Shayna Potts

I feel like I live in a window at the mall.
Every minute of the day
Everyone watches
Every move I make,
And I hate the way I look.
    My legs are too long,
    My eyes are too big,
    And my hair is entirely too curly.

    I'd rather be a roach,
    And live under a stove
    Where no one would ever see me.

    I'd rather be a worm,
    And live in a garden
    Under six feet of dirt,
    Too deep to ever be found.

    I'd rather be a germ,
    And live in the belly of a whale,
    At the bottom of an ocean,
    On a planet in a universe
    A thousand light years away.

Every minute of the day
Everyone watches
Every… move… I make.

Emma's Dilemma
by Emma Mackey

His name is C.J.
And I really like him,
But it would be dishonest to keep going out with him,
Because I don't like him the way he likes me,
But there's a problem,
Because he's a freshman
And his winter formal's in two weeks
And if I break up with him now
He won't have a date
So I have to stick with him until after his formal.

But today Lauren told me
He's going to give me a gold chain,
And if I don't take it
Everybody will say I'm mean to him,
And if I do take it
I'll be stuck with him forever.
It could be a whole month,
And that would be mean to me,
So it's like I'm in a trap
And there's absolutely no way out.

His name is C.J.,
My name is Emma,
And our love has become
A disturbing dilemma.

Left Out
by Juan Carlos Hernandez

I don't think they do it on purpose,
But it happens all the time.
They leave me out.
  Friday night they went to the movies,
  But nobody told me about it.
  Saturday morning they played basketball,
  But no one told me where.
  Then Saturday night they ordered pizza
  And watched scary movies on cable,
  But I wasn't invited.
So I sit alone in my room at home
And think,
And hope,
Maybe they don't do it on purpose.

Bored
by Steven Gilley

Forty-three stations on the radio,
Ninety-seven channels on cable TV,
Thirty-nine thousand books in the library,
And the whole world on the Internet.
So why am I totally bored?

I'm lying in bed, I smell like cheese,
And half the day is through.
I think I get so bored because
There's too much stuff to do.

Black Hole Brain

by Shayna Potts

It happened again,
In the middle of Science class
Mr. Grindle was talking about black holes,
How they're all over the universe
But you can't see them
Because they suck up everything around them
Even rays of light,
And I started thinking:
> If only I had a black hole
> I'd never rake the lawn.
> I'd throw that hole out on the grass
> And the leaves would all be gone.

And the fun I'd have at school!
I'd roll it down the hall,
And that hole would suck up everything,
Teachers, books, and all.

I must have laughed out loud,
Because the next thing I heard
Was the voice of Mr. Grindle:
    "Well now, Miss Potts,
    If it's that funny,
    Please…
    Don't be selfish,
    Why don't you share it with the rest of us."

It happens all the time,
It happens every day.
My wild imagination
Simply steals my brain away.

"Most black holes are far away,
But some are close," I said.
"I know because I think there's one
Stuck right here in my head."

The Sound of Stink
by Christina Curtis

It happens every day:
The bell rings,
Lunch is over,
We're off to fifth period.
And there they are,
Right in the front row,
The stinky trio —
    Angelo Caesar,
    Eric Hansen,
    And Aaron Bell.

The teacher enters,
Begins to lecture,
And, with the predictability of the planets,
They start:
    Angelo begins with a baritone rumble,
    Eric joins in with a treble toot,
    Followed by Aaron's long, deep, bass blast.

It's another afternoon of body gas.
A series of atmospheric insults
Followed by the giggles of near full-grown men.

After the first time it shouldn't be funny,
At least that's what you'd think.
What is it that makes people laugh
At the sound of human stink?

AAAUGH!

Published
by Juan Carlos Hernandez

In the middle of Math class
Angelina handed me a heart-shaped note,
But Ms. Anderson saw it.
"What have we here?" she cackled
As she took the note from my hand.

I should have said something.
I should have said,
"That is a personal communication.
Please respect my privacy
And return that note immediately."
But no!
I sat like a rock and listened
As she began to read out loud:

> *"Oh Carlos, my Carlos, I love you.*
> *I love you more than life itself,*
> *I love you with a love that will last forever.*
> *With a heart full of kisses, I am*
> *   Your Angelina"*

I thought I'd be embarrassed,
But as I heard the words
My heart began to grow.
Angelina loves me,
And I want the world to know.

Counter Intelligence

by Christina Curtis

It's hard to believe
But this is exactly what he said:
    "We boys are so much smarter than girls.
    Like last week,
    When Courtney sent a note to Rachel,
    We knew it was a big secret,
    Because on the outside she wrote:

        GIRLS' EYES ONLY
        NO BOYS ALLOWED!
        ESPECIALLY BILLY CARTER

    But that didn't stop us.
    Peter got Kelly to talk to Katrina,
    Who's best friends with Courtney's best friend Rachel,
    And she told us everything that was in that note,
        How Courtney thinks Billy's so cute,
        And how she wants to go out with him.
    So we told Billy all about it
    And Billy asked Courtney to meet him at the mall,
    And now Courtney and Billy are going together.
    You see! That proves it!
    Boys are totally smarter than girls."
I listened to every word he said
And when he was finally through,
I thought to myself, "You poor little boys,
You haven't got a clue."

The Valentine Wimp

by Benjamin Talkington Sprock, III

I really like Marilou,
So I put pen to paper
And wrote the perfect valentine:
> *These simple words my heart must say,*
> *I cannot wait another day.*
> *This heart so full of love divine,*
> *For you, my darling Valentine.*

But then I started to wonder,
Does she feel the same about me?
What if she shows it to her friends
And laughs behind my back?

My pounding heart is warm with love,
My brain is cold with fear,
So I'll just keep this valentine
And try again next year.

The Question Mark
(An Unusual Homework Assignment)

by Shayna Potts

English class! A bottomless pit!
Darkness without spark!
"If the sentence is asking a question," she says,
"End with a question mark."

I know how to use a question mark,
I'm a punctuation pro.
So why can't she just teach me
The things I need to know?

Like how do I do my lipstick?
And how do I walk in heels?
And when I have to kiss a boy,
How is it going to feel?

So there—I've done my assignment,
The coolest I ever had:
"Write sixteen lines of poetry
That'll make your teacher mad."

Underarm Charm

by Ryan Spalding

Last night at the drugstore,
My mother smiled discreetly and said:
"Look, Ryan, deodorant.
Would you like the roll-on or the spray?"

I may not have big muscles,
And I may not have a tan,
But I'm growing hairy armpits,
And I'm smelling like a man.

Old Friends

Steven and I continued throughout the seventh grade to work together on the editing committee. Our efforts to get others to help were a dismal failure, so for two to three hours a week we sat alone at a table in the library and read the newly submitted poems. As I began to know Steven better, I really enjoyed his company. We sometimes talked about other things besides poetry, and I discovered that for all his goofiness and obnoxious teasing, he was really a very serious person.

It was during one of these conversations in the last weeks of school that I said to him, "Have you noticed that most of the poems submitted to us are funny? Maybe we should be writing more serious poetry."

As if on cue, Steven grinned back at me and broke into a recitation:

> "I have seen roses damasked, red and white,
> But no such roses see I in her cheeks;
> And in some perfumes is there more delight
> Than in the breath that from my mistress reeks."

"Reeks!" I cried, certain the boy had finally flipped. "What are you talking about?"

"It's Shakespeare," he said, "Sonnet #130, as a matter of fact, and it's funny! For hundreds of years poets had been writing smoochy stuff about their girlfriends and Shakespeare decided to make fun of it. But at the end of the poem he says:

> 'And yet, by heaven, I think my love as rare
> As any she belied with false compare.'

"You see, Christina, he's telling his girlfriend that she isn't perfect, but it's okay, because she doesn't have to be perfect for him." Then looking at me intensely, minus the usual mischievous smile, he added, "He loves her just the way she is."

I guess I blushed, but I remember how baffled I was by the Mr. Serious across from me. Where did this Steven come from? He must have read the look on my face, because he leaned over and whispered, "Several years ago I spent a long time in the hospital. It was a very confusing time, and I was afraid I might not get the chance to do some of the things in life I wanted to do." Then he suddenly stopped talking, stared at me, and without saying another word, grabbed his book bag and walked out of the library.

What did I do? I wondered. *Why did he leave like that?*

School ended a couple weeks later and we went our separate ways. Over the summer I often wondered what happened in the library and felt disappointed that Steven either didn't like or trust me enough to finish what he had begun to tell me.

On the first day of eighth grade everyone was happy to see each other again. I immediately scanned the groups of boys in search of Steven. I couldn't wait to see him, but he was nowhere to be found. I was told he spent June and July with his father in Oregon, so I figured he was probably just late getting back. But he didn't show up the next day, or the next. A week went by, then another, and pretty soon it was October and no one seemed to know what happened to him.

Then one day in mid-October, I turned a corner by the biology lab and almost walked right passed him—he looked so different. Steven was almost completely bald and my first reaction was to laugh thinking he had shaved his head. But as I looked closer I realized his hair had fallen out. He was thin, and unlike the rest of us who still had our summer suntans, Steven was pale—very pale. I felt so embarrassed for him. But, true to form, Steven gave me that silly Gilley smile and said he'd meet me after school.

Our schoolyard was mostly asphalt, but there was a patch of grass around this really old maple tree and that's where we met. Steven was sitting on the ground against the tree with a leaf in his hand, one of those reddish-orange leaves that make trees so beautiful in autumn.

"So thoughtful," I said as I sat beside him.

"This isn't easy," he said. "I've wanted to tell you lots of times but it's such a bummer." Then his voice became very soft. "I've got leukemia, Christina. I've had it since fourth grade. They thought I wouldn't live through the treatments, but I've been in remission now for a few years. Remission doesn't mean you're cured, only that you're better. This summer I started to get sick again and that's why I was late returning to school and why I look this way."

I swallowed hard and tried not to stare at him. I didn't know what to say or where to look. If I look at his hair, I thought, it might make him feel uncomfortable. If I look at his eyes, I'll start to cry. I turned and saw a group of girls staring at us and whispering so I stared back at them as if to say, *Beat it!*

He sensed that I was upset. "Everybody's got to die someday," he said, "it's just that most people don't think about it. The difference with me is that I don't get to pretend I'm going to live forever."

I'll never forget how composed he was, sitting there with that leaf in his hands. It was as though we were sitting in a pocket of calm; a stillness that came from Steven and wrapped itself around the two of us.

"When I found out I was sick, I was pretty upset. All I could think about was dying. And I had a million questions—the kind of questions that don't come with easy answers. Why do some people die when they're young, and why me, and why was I born anyway? My dad teaches philosophy so I got out one of his books, but I couldn't even understand the first page.

"I asked him to help me and he said I might be looking in the wrong place. Then he showed me a poem by a guy who died when he was real young. He didn't read the whole thing; just the last two lines about beauty and truth. I didn't know why but I felt a little better and every night after that we read poetry together."

"So that's how you know so much about poetry," I exclaimed. "That's how you know so many poems by heart."

"Exactly," he said. "We read tons of poems. Some of them were pretty awful but some of them were good."

"Did you find the answers you were looking for?"

"No, I didn't, but I found some friends, like Emily Dickinson. She knew all about loneliness and the feelings of darkness inside of us. I read a few of her poems and they were okay, but then I found this poem called 'I Died for Beauty.' I liked it a lot and read it over and over, and pretty soon I knew it by heart. Whenever I felt lonely I'd recite it. At first it was only my own voice saying the words in my head, but then I started to hear her voice whispering the words to me. It was like she was my friend and had written the words just for me.

"Then came Robert Frost's 'Stopping by Woods on a Snowy Evening,' and I started to hear his voice, too. There were lots of others and they were like real people, people I knew. I even gave them nicknames—'Sweet Emmy' for Emily Dickinson, 'Bobby the Grouch' for Robert Frost, 'Boss Bill' for Shakespeare.

"It didn't exactly make everything great, but after a while I didn't feel so alone anymore, and I don't feel lonely now because the poets are with me all the time—when I'm happy they laugh with me, when I'm angry I remember that they were angry too, and when I'm scared to die, death doesn't seem so dark because they've all gone before me."

COUNTY PUBLIC LIBRARY

"Do you remember the poem you started with, those lines about truth and beauty?" I asked.

"Sure," he said, "it's from a poem called 'Ode to a Grecian Urn' by John Keats. He's looking at this old Greek vase with pictures on it. One of the pictures is of a boy and a girl sitting under a tree just like we are right now, and he's thinking about how those scenes have been frozen in time for over two thousand years, and at the end he says:

'When old age shall this generation waste,
    Thou shalt remain, in midst of other woe
Than ours, a friend to man, to whom thou say'st,
    'Beauty is truth, truth beauty,—that is all
Ye know on earth, and all ye need to know.'"

Then he took my hand in his, opened my fingers, and placed the maple leaf on my palm. "This leaf," he said, "was a bud last spring, all summer it was green, and now it's finished. That's truth. But look at it, Christina, look how beautiful it is. It's like that all around us and that's why I feel so lucky. Some people live a hundred years and never notice how beautiful it is, how beautiful it is to be alive."

Steven Gilley was alive, and he stayed that way. He grew stronger every day, and by Christmas he was back to the most unbearably immature, totally annoying boy in the world. But I knew better. I knew the real Steven Gilley, and he was becoming my best friend.

Our Eighth Grade Poems

The Umbilical Ring
by Shayna Potts

It was last summer
   And I was grounded for lying to my mother
   And my mother was finally starting to give in
   And she let me go to the coffee house
   And I ran into this guy who's a friend of mine
   And he's really just a friend
   And we were totally bored,
   And he knew a guy who did piercing
   And so I said "Why not?"
   And the piercing-guy had these awesome navel rings
   And I've got such a cute little navel
   So I said to myself *DO IT!*

Later I was really scared,
And when my mother eventually saw it
I thought I was fried
But what was her reaction?
   "Oh Shayna!
   "It's so cute!"

And now it's totally marvelous,
The very coolest of things,
It's mother-daughter navels
With matching navel rings.

In My Time of Need

by Benjamin Talkington Sprock, III

Dear Lord,
I ain't asking much,
And it's okay if she ain't pretty,
Well maybe she could be a little pretty,
Or at least not too ugly,
But Lord,
I really need a girl.
    A girl who'll smile when she sees me,
    And sigh when she says goodnight.
    A girl who'll whisper my name
    Like the words of a prayer.
Please listen, Lord,
I ain't asking the world,
But please, do you think
You could send me a girl?

What Goes Around

by Gerald T. Simpson

Last year
Brandi and Ryan were going out,
But Ryan got bored,
So on the last day of school,
Ryan dumped her,
And Brandi cried.

Now it's a brand new year,
And Brandi's not crying anymore,
Because this year
Brandi is a B-A-B-E! Babe!
The guys are going crazy.
And Ryan?

That boy done lost his appetite.
He's looking mighty thin.
The wheel of life has turned and now
It's Brandi's turn to win.

Chicken Leg's Revenge
by Christina Curtis

Meagan's a new girl at school,
And yesterday at gym class,
She was wearing these baby blue shorts,
And that girl has got some chicken legs.
I mean two long, seriously skinny legs,
And that's all Calvin Keating needed.
He started flapping his elbows like a chicken
Clucking and scratching at the floor.
And in two seconds,
Every boy in class was clucking like a chicken
And laughing at Meagan.

I have always hated gym class.
You try wearing shorts around the guys in our school.
As I watched Calvin and his buddies,
I thought —
 Poor Meagan,
 Your first day of school
 And look what these fools have done to you.

But Meagan was spectacular.
She didn't sigh, she didn't cry,
But oh what a display!
She walked up to Calvin, pulled down his shorts,
And chicken-clucked away.

Line in the Dirt
by Isabela Galindo

I always try to be nice to you.
    I bake you brownies,
    I tutor you in math,
    I go to your boring baseball games.
I do these things because I like you.

But you are seldom nice to me.
    You're never on time,
    You forget to call when you say you will,
    You do not listen when I speak.
You do these things out of habit,
And because you think only of yourself.

So I am drawing a line in the dirt,
Or else I might explode.
You better decide to treat me nice
Or buster, hit the road!

Word to the Wise
by Bobby Hall

In the middle of the lunchroom,
Lindsey McDonald got out of her chair,
Looked me right in the eye,
And threw down the challenge.
    "You think you're hot stuff
    Cause you're a big football player.
    Well I can play football too,
    And I'm saying it,
    Right here and now,
    I'll out-run you,

I'll out-pass you,
And I'll stomp you in the ground like a pancake."
That's what she said,
And me, poor sucker that I am,
I said, "Oh yeah!
I'd like to see you try."
And everybody followed us outside
To see what would happen.

I could tell you how I slaughtered her,
But it would all be lies,
And so instead from this hospital bed,
I offer a word to the wise:

Some girls primp,
Some girls strut,
Some girls flirt,
And some KICK BUTT!

HOSPITAL.

Just a Friend

by Amy Hays

He's just a friend.
    Sure the other girls think he's cute,
    And yes I do sort of like being around him,
    And I admit, when he walks in a room,
    My hands begin to tremble,
    My lips begin to quiver,
    I can hardly catch my breath,
    And I want to throw myself at his feet and scream:
    "I am your woman!
    Your slave!
    Your companion for life!
    I will bear your children!
    I will be your wife!"
But really…
He's just a friend.

Mi Hermano el Marrano

by Juan Carlos Hernandez

My big brother is a pig.
Cada día de la semana, he kicks my butt.
En el fin de semana, he kicks my butt.
Mañana, tarde, y noche, he kicks my butt.

But today there was a new girl at school,
Her name is Felicia,
And for the first time in my life,
¡Hay esperanza!
Porque Felicia likes me.
And Felicia said she would do anything I ask.
¿Y Felicia? ¡Esa niña es muy grande y muy fuerte!
So today I asked Felicia for one small favor.
    "O Felicia, mi novia, mi amor,
    Esta vez nada mas,
    Felicia, por favor,
    Kick my brother's butt!"

Yes, my brother's a pig,
Muy macho y con bravado,
But thanks to my girlfriend Felicia,
Ahora es jamón asado.

Map Manipulation
by Shayna Potts

Today we learned our map-skills:
    Latitude, longitude,
    The International Dateline,
    And the perennial Prime Meridian.
I thought it was totally boring.

But then our teacher explained
That the world doesn't really begin at Greenwich, England,
That some scientist drew a line there,
Wrote a zero next to that line,
And declared it the Prime Meridian.
And I thought, that is really interesting.
Because
    A) If the Prime Meridian was *arbitrarily* placed
        It can be *arbitrarily* moved.
And
    B) If the Prime Meridian can be *arbitrarily* moved
        The International Dateline can be *arbitrarily* moved as well.

So I erased the International Dateline,
And repositioned it on a north-south line
That runs smack in the middle of my classroom.
So that now,
When geography class gets boring again,
I will simply step across my personal International Dateline
Moving boldly into tomorrow,
And escaping the boring geography lesson
That will be happening at that very moment,
Yesterday,
On the other side of the classroom.

Studying maps is boring and cruel,
But tormenting teachers is totally cool.

Lies, More Lies, and a Moment of Truth

by Benjamin Talkington Sprock, III

Your blaze of brain and body,
The fire in your eyes,
It grills my heart with fire
And fills my mouth with lies.

The shining lock of raven black,
Blown free across your face —
A mystic twirl that lights my world
And warms my inner space.

It just comes out this way
No matter what I do.
And it may not sound sincere
But it's really almost true.

That blinding flash of intellect,
Your burning need to know,
Your strength of voice compels my choice,
I'm drawn into your glow.

I want it to sound romantic
But then I start to fear,
The words are all so flowery
It comes out insincere.

That's why I wrote this poem,
I wanted you to see,
If all the world had just one girl
You'd be that girl for me.

Glory and Defeat
by Bobby Hall

The opening kickoff,
I take it at the twenty,
A hole opens to my right.
I find a lane down the sideline,
I'm in the clear at the thirty,
I can smell the goal.
A thousand voices roar at the glory of my athletic ability,
And that sound is the last thing I remember.

That was Friday night.
It's Saturday morning now,
And Nurse Attila the Hun just read me the sports page,
    How their kicker,
      Their one hundred thirty-two pound kicker,
      Obliterated the home team's star running back
      On the opening kickoff.

Attila the Hun says it's a very old story —
"One person's pain is another one's glory."

Makeover Man
by Amy Hays

I am excited,
I am happy,
I am dancing on air,
Because I, Amy Hays,
Have finally got a boyfriend
And he's *so* fine!

But now it's time to get to work,
Because those T-shirts he wears are a mess,
He's going to have to cut that hair,
And that ring in his nose has got to go.

I really love him for what he is
And I'll never try to change him.
A woman should never change her man . . .
But it's her job to rearrange him.

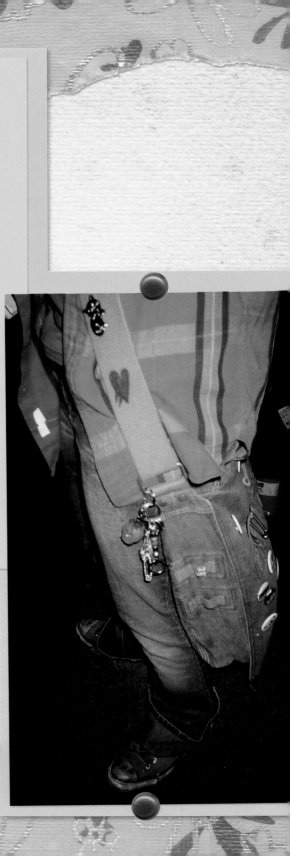

Dawn at Sunset

by Ryan Spalding

For seven years
She lived in the house next door
But I never paid much attention,
Until this evening.

I turned my bicycle into the driveway
Glanced across the lawn,
And there she was, Dawn Marie Simpson.
And it was as though I had never seen her before:
    Her hair, black as darkest night,
    Her eyes, bright as morning sun,
    The movement of her body
    Like the roll of waves on ocean swirl.
Yes, I had discovered Dawn Marie
And I wanted her to discover me,
And I wanted to look real cool,
So I stood up on the peddles of my bicycle,
Real nonchalant like,
(As I continued to roll toward the garage door)
And called out,
"Yo, Dawn!
What's happening, girl!"

Today I learned that my driveway is short,
And I learned life can be cruel,
And I learned I should first get off of my bike
Before I try to look cool.

Daze of the Weak

by Shayna Potts

Monday morning — slow motion pain.
Tuesday was a bear.
Wednesday wasn't all that bad,
I'd made it half-way there.

Thursday's tests and book reports.
My teacher thinks it's fun
To bury us with projects
And give homework by the ton.

So now, at last, it's Friday night
And my body feels like lead,
All my friends went straight to the mall,
But I just went to bed.

I'm way too tired to talk on the phone
Too tired to even speak.
The joyful days of my childhood
Have turned into the daze of the weak.

(handwritten insurance card illustration)

♥ Insurance Breakup Card IBC

Member Name Emma Mackey

Member ID BU411

Group number 231-Breakup

Date to breakup _____

Victim - boyfriend

Customer Service # - 1800- Breakup NOW!

40

Heartbreak Insurance

by Emma Mackey

We'd been going out for an entire week
And whenever I thought of him I felt warm inside,
And when I was with him
My stomach tingled,
And last night at the mall,
As I turned the corner and saw him walking toward me,
My face wanted to burst into smile.
But instead I said:
    "Michael, it's over.
    Please don't ask me to explain,
    It's just over.
    Period!"
And I walked away.

It always hurts when it's time to break up,
But if a guy breaks up with me
It hurts a whole lot worse,
And that is why, as a matter of insurance,
I always break up first.

Alfredo y Marco

by Isabela Galindo

Marco thinks he's cool,
Just because he's good looking.
He struts around school like a rooster
And talks to girls as if we were slaves:
"Yo, baby,
Let me copy your homework."

"Yo, baby,
Loan me a dollar."

"Yo, baby! Yo, baby! Yo, baby!"

And Alfredo,
He is not very good looking,
But he's so sweet,
And he treats girls as if each of us were a princess:

"Karla,
Your hair,
Looking good!"

"Alana please!
Let me help you with that backpack,
A girl like you should float like an angel."

Alfredo y Marco,
Two boys at our school.
Alfredo is sweet,
And Marco's a fool.

Marco is handsome
But he's so immature,
Alfredo es feo,
Pero es mi amor.

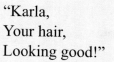

Low-Down, Two-Timing Scum-Sucker

by Emma Mackey

Sylvia's my best friend,
And her face was aglow
As she began to speak,
But when the words came out of her mouth
I could hardly believe my ears:
    "Benjamin called me last night," she sighed,
    "He said he loved me
    And that he'll never love another.
    He even called me his angel face."

The Benjamin to whom she referred
Was none other than Benjamin Talkington Sprock the Third!
And last night,
I too had a conversation with Mr. Sprock,
And in that conversation:
    He told *me* how much he loved me,
    And he told *me* he would never love another,
    And apparently *I too* am Benjamin's angel face.

So Sylvia and I had a little talk,
And today after school
She and I will walk side by side
To the big house at the corner of Main,
The home of a certain Benjamin Talkington Sprock,
Where we shall ascend the steps,
Ring the bell,
And wait for Benjamin to come to the door.

That low-down, two-timing scum-sucker
Will think he's seeing double.
Benjamin doesn't know it yet,
But the boy's in a heap of trouble.

Dream Kiss

by Steven Gilley

She steps toward me . . .
Parts her lips . . .
And touches them to mine.

They say to live in dreams
Is a foolish thing to do,
But someday, if I dream enough,
Someday it might come true.

Respiratory Failure

by Emma Mackey

Today we studied the respiratory system:
    The diaphragm contracts,
    Air moves through the esophagus into the lungs,
    Where alveolar blood gathers oxygen,
    Flows up the pulmonary artery,
    Through the heart
    And out to the rest of the body.
Today we studied the respiratory system
And mine was working fine
Until Derrick Wood walked up to me and said hello,
And as I gazed into his eyes,
    My diaphragm did not contract,
    No air flowed through my esophagus,
    My alveoli took a vacation,
    And my body screamed for oxygen.
I'm feeling better now,
But I've got one thing to say:
Derrick Wood, you hunk of man,
You take my breath away!

Pom-Pom Poison

by Isabela Galindo

I think I've finally figured out
That cheerleaders are very dangerous people,
Like last night at the Valentine Dance:
    Sharon Sims,
    With her shiny blond hair,
    And her sparkling blue eyes,
    And her personality bubbling
    Like Alka-Seltzer in a punch bowl.
    The very same Sharon Sims
    Who slithered across the floor
    And poisoned my boyfriend
    With the venom of her cheerleader smiles.
Sharon Sims, a lovely girl,
But please make no mistake,
That peachy little pom-pom girl's
More dangerous than a snake.

Imperfect Me

by Christina Curtis

I used to try to be perfect:
    Perfect height, perfect weight,
    A perfect friend, the perfect date,
    Perfect makeup on my face
    Every hair in perfect place.
    The perfect mask for all to see,
    I tried to be a perfect me.
But I couldn't do it:
    I'm short and just a little plump,
    My nose has got a tiny bump,
    My teeth? Too big. My ears? Too long.
    The me I see is always wrong.
    I felt such animosity,
    My life was an atrocity.
But then I wised up:
    Perfect looks? A total scam!
    Perfection lies in who I am.
    This girl has got one life to live
    And who I am is what I give,
    And if I give with all my might
    The me I give will be just right.

And suddenly my heart broke free
So here I am — Imperfect Me.

The Door Unopened

By Emma Mackey

In our house there are doors—
    A front door,
    A back door,
    A door to the patio.
Doors that open to the light.

But there's another door—
    A door that moves on rusty hinges
    To steps that sink through silence,
    Past the whisper of broken promises,
    Into the dust of forbidden memory.
In my house there are lots of doors,
And among them
There is one door
I can never open again.

The Brightest Star
by Steven Gilley

Last night,
In the field behind my house,
I sat on the grass and watched the stars —
   A zillion sparkles
   That turned the sky
   Into an ocean of floating fire.
And low on the southern horizon,
Just above the trees,
There burned a star so bright,
That all the others seemed dim.
And it made me think of you,
Christina strong and tall,
Of all the girls who ever lived,
The brightest star of all.

An Unnamed Star

The last few months of eighth grade were very emotional; it was "the last time" for everything.

"This is the last April Fool's Day we'll have in middle school."

"These are our last mid-terms."

It got so ridiculous we started making fun of ourselves. "This could be the last time we eat corn in the cafeteria."

"That could be the very last time we hear Andrew cut the cheese in Spanish class."

It was absolutely juvenile and we enjoyed every moment of it. But as graduation drew near, we weren't laughing quite as much. It was Ashley Huffman who dramatized what lots of us were feeling.

"Three years ago, like children at the beginning of a tunnel, we entered middle school," she said with a sigh. "For three long years we have stumbled in the dark, and now, as we emerge from the other end, we are adults." Ashley never lost her touch for dramatic exaggeration. We weren't exactly children when we started, it wasn't always so dark, and when we graduated we weren't totally adult. But we had come a long way and we'd done it together.

The last day of school was an emotional roller coaster. Wildly happy yet always on the verge of tears, we inscribed each other's yearbooks with pledges of eternal friendship and made our goodbyes. Steven Gilley, who never missed an opportunity to make fun of serious emotions, absolutely outdid himself.

He'd walk up to a group of girls, fold his hands over his heart, and begin to recite this very sentimental poem he'd written for the occasion:

Now we all must go away
Never to come back this way,
Happy days have reached the end,
Good friends may never meet again.

The reaction was always the same. First the girls would turn to each other and start hugging and sobbing. Then Steven would scream with laughter and the girls would pound on him until he ran away in search of another group to torment.

Steven and I met that afternoon for the last time at our table in the poetry section of the library. "There's something I want to say to you," he began. "I've wanted to say it for a long time but I always chickened out." He looked real serious and for a second I thought he was about to recite that stupid poem, but he didn't, and I'm glad I didn't interrupt him.

"For a long time I didn't know it myself," he continued, "not until last summer when I had to go through that treatment again. The medicine they give you makes you sick, really sick, so sick that sometimes you want to give up, like it doesn't matter if you live another day. I only felt that way a few times, but whenever it happened it was you that got me through it. I'd imagine you as Athena the Warrior Goddess. You'd walk up to my bed, look down at me and shout, 'Get up out of that bed, you slime, and stop feeling sorry for yourself.' It was kind of funny and it really helped me."

I was holding a pencil in my hand and, as he began to talk so seriously, I twirled it over and over slowly between my fingers. Steven reached out and, barely touching my hand, stopped the pencil. Then, almost as though he'd rehearsed it, he took my hand between both of his and looked directly into my eyes.

"Now please don't get all geeky about this," he said, "but that's when I realized that I love you. I love you for being strong. I love you for being smart. I love the way you smile when you understand something for the first time. And I love the way you make me feel when I'm with you. So there, I had to tell you. Wouldn't it have been terrible if you were the only girl I ever loved and I never told you? So I've said it. I just wanted you to know."

I kept thinking—does he mean it? Is he kidding? Is he about to make a joke?

I was speechless, and before I could say anything, Steven pushed back his chair, grabbed his books, and rushed out of the library.

I saw him again later that day but it was from a distance. He was reciting to a group of weeping girls:

> "Now we all must go away
> Never to come back this way,
> Happy days have reached the end,
> Good friends may never meet again."

A lot has happened since then—four years of high school and a whole lot of growing up. My dad says we're at a time in our lives when we're old enough to dream big dreams and young enough to believe them. I think he's right. Some of us are dreaming some pretty big dreams:

Bobby Hall got a scholarship to play college football and he's hoping he'll make it to the NFL.

Ashley Huffman has her whole future figured out. She'll study communications, start out as a local TV reporter, and eventually become a network news anchor. Isn't that perfect! Ashley's flair for dramatic exaggeration should send her right to the top in the news business.

Ryan Spalding is doing standup comedy. All he does is talk about the crazy stuff that actually happens to him and everybody laughs.

After middle school, Steven went to live with his dad and attended high school in Oregon. For a while, we emailed almost every day, but you know how that is. Pretty soon it was once a week, then once a month, then hardly ever. Then, toward the end of sophomore year, he sent me a poem. I was amazed to see how he'd grown as a writer.

He said he'd been reading about the stars, how there are billions of them and most of them don't even have names; the astronomers just give them numbers and identify them by their coordinates in the sky. He said it reminded him of himself and me and all the other Digital Poets.

The Voice of an Unnamed Star

by Steven Gilley

You will find me
Past the Prime Meridian
At eighteen hours seven minutes four.

You will find me
Beneath the celestial equator
By twenty-three degrees forty-five minutes
And not one second more.

Ruled by Jupiter,
The warm and wise,
I am but a sparkle in the eye of the archer,
A speck in the cloud of the Milky Way,
So small beside these giants of the universe.
And yet,
A line drawn through me from the center of the Sun
Will pierce the heart of a galaxy.
And so,
In this ocean of eternal night,
I make day.
I burn to give this light away
And in burning earn the right to say
I am a star.

So, in the twilight of some cool September evening,
Remember me,
And perceiving how I loved you,
Look for me again,
Just above the southern horizon,
For I will be there,
And you will find me.

STEVEN
GILLEY

I read the poem and liked it very much. Then I read it again and liked it even more. Then I read it a third time and I knew that something was wrong. It was the part where he said, "So in the twilight of some cool September evening/ Remember me . . . ." It was like he knew he was going away—really going away.

We hadn't talked to each other for a long time. As I dialed the phone, I hoped it was still a good number. Steven's father answered and when Steven came on the line his voice was weak.

We talked about Athena and Thor and the Digital Poets and how Mrs. Zimmerman always stood up for us. We talked about some of the wild-man things Mr. Barker did when he recited poems, and how we wished someone had videotaped it so we could see it again. We talked about leaving middle school and wondered what might have happened if he hadn't moved to Oregon. We talked for over an hour, and when it seemed as though there was nothing left to talk about, I took a deep breath.

"Steven," I said, "remember that day in the library when you told me that you loved me?"

There was silence on the other end of the line, but I pushed forward anyway. "Well, I haven't forgotten it, and I don't think I'll ever forget it— the way you said you loved me and the reasons you gave. Don't think I'm saying this now just because you've become a really good poet," I said teasingly, "but as I read your poem I realized there was something I have wanted to tell you for a long time.

"Now please don't get all geeky about this," I said, "but what I realized is that I love you. I love you for being strong. I love you for being smart. I love the way you smile when you understand something for the first time. And I love the way you make me feel when I'm with you. So there, I had to tell you. Wouldn't it have been terrible if you were the only boy I ever loved and I never even told you? So I've said it. I just wanted you to know."

After that we emailed every day. As time went by his messages grew shorter. And then I received this message from his father:

```
Sent: Wednesday, May 1: 10:57 AM
Subject: Steven Gilley

Steven passed away at 9 am this
morning, May 1st, after a long,
difficult struggle, with his mom and
dad by his side, in his own room,
in his own bed.
```

That's when I put the Digital Poets scrapbook in the bottom of my closet. It was too painful to remember. But now I want to remember, and I can because I have his poems.

My favorite is his last one, the one about the unknown star. To me it isn't just a poem. It's the voice of a real person who lived and died, a voice inside me when I'm happy or angry or scared, a voice that's with me all the time, so I never have to be alone. I've read it so often I know it by heart. At first, as I said the words, the voice I heard was my own, but then it became Steven's voice, the voice of a poet who was my friend, a poet who loved me; an unnamed star that burned to make a glimmer of light in a world of darkness.

An Afterthought

So that's the story of the Digital Poets. Everything is so different now. The middle school children we used to be aren't around anymore, but we put ourselves into our poems and now we've shared them with you.

And who knows, maybe you'll do it too. Just start writing. Then, when you can no longer remember what it was like to be young, you'll have your poems to remind you—a personal time machine to bring you back to before. And remember, to be a star you don't have to be rich or famous. You need only open your heart, just a little, so the fire inside you can make a little bit of light in a universe of darkness.

I have one more poem for you. It was a handout from Mr. Barker. He said he liked it and wanted to pass it on to us. I like it too, so I'm passing it on to you.

Christina Curtis

The ABC Song
by Brod Bagert

A is for answers,
In life there are few.
B is for bodies,
Soon old though once new.
C is for creep…
As time creeps surely by.
And D?
D is for dog.

E is for ears
To hear the soft voices.
F is for folly
In all of life's choices.
G is for goodness,
My goodness! My gracious!
And H is simply for hog.

I J K L — In Jeweled Kingdoms of Love.
M N O ? Man knows Not Of.

P is for peace,
Q is for quiet,
R is for reasons
To fall off your diet.
S is for sin,
T, your turn to win,
U, unforgivable you.

V and W
X Y and Z,
I am old and I'm tired,
Please don't listen to me.
Go climb some tall mountain
Or sail the big sea.
U, irreplaceable you.

Live each moment,
Not its future or past.
There once was a first
And will soon be a last.
Like the alphabet song
Life begins and it ends,
So sing out each letter my children,
Sing loudly each letter, my friends.

"Who Wrote What" Index

+ 20 years = supermodel

Steven

Shayna Potts
Great Minds
Torture Queen
No Reason at All
Aunt Aurora's Promise
Freedom of Speech
Yellow Bus Blues
Inner Eye
Black Hole Brain
The Question Mark
The Umbilical Ring
Map Manipulation
Daze of the Weak

Gerald T. Simpson
Twenty-Five Hours
Man Fan
What Goes Around

Ryan Spalding
Lips
The Girl-Crazy Alien Body Snatcher
Jungle of Love
Underarm Charm
Dawn at Sunset

Benjamin Talkington Sprock, III
Planning for the Future
The Hunt
Unwritten Rules
The Valentine Wimp
In My Time of Need
Lies, More Lies, and a Moment of Truth

In Memory of My Wonderful Niece

Rebecca Claire Fakier

The Brightest Star

Acknowledgments

This book began nine years ago when the irrepressible Cathy Barker asked me to write poems for her sixth graders, who soon became an ongoing source of inspiration and unflinching criticism. They explained to me that my characters' names were terrible and insisted that I use their names instead. To both teacher and students, I send a huge thank you.

Thanks also to Michael Zimmerman and his Illinois sixth graders. At one point, in frustration, I decided to delete the story part of this book and publish instead a simple collection of poems. Mr. Zimmerman's students told me I was making a big mistake and that I'd simply have to find a way to make the story work.

Thanks to my son John David and to his New Orleans classmates who, back in seventh and eighth grade, read my poems, graded them, and helped me learn to stay on course.

Thanks to Janet Boltges, a high school librarian, who drove me to a South Carolina arts and crafts store and introduced me to the world of scrapbooks.

Thanks to the artists in Alexandria Zettler's middle school art class for their wonderful drawings and the authenticity they bring to Christina's scrapbook.

Thanks to my editor, Erica Nikolaidis, for bringing Christina's scrapbook to life.

And thanks to my publisher, Julia Graddy, for believing in my work.

About the Artists

The original artwork in *Hormone Jungle* was created by the following middle school students in Alexandria Zettler's art class at PK Yonge Laboratory School in Gainesville, Florida:

Alexandria Zettler

Corey Barnes

Daisy Mason

Daphne Flournoy

Dinah Mason

Emily Walsh

Erica Wiggins

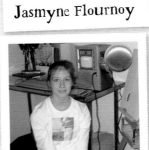

Jasmyne Flournoy

Joseph Pauly

Robin Waters

Tessa Paulsen

Tiara Luckie

About the Author

Brod Bagert's poetry captures a myriad of voices that speak to adults and children alike. Brod visits schools and conferences across America promoting performance as the best way to teach poetry. He is also the author of ten books of poetry, including *Rainbows, Head Lice, and Pea-Green Tile* (Maupin House, 1999), a collection of poems written in the voice of the classroom teacher, and *Giant Children* (Dial, 2004), which was nominated for the 2005 K-3 Children's Choice Award.